Sandy to the Rescue!

by Rose Lin
Illustrated by Laura Gibbons Nickeil

PEARSON
Scott Foresman

Editorial Offices: Glenview, Illinois • Parsippany, New Jersey • New York, New York
Sales Offices: Needham, Massachusetts • Duluth, Georgia • Glenview, Illinois
Coppell, Texas • Sacramento, California • Mesa, Arizona

Sandy is a dog. She lives with Kim. Kim is taking Sandy to her lesson. Sandy is learning how to find people who are lost. Sandy will be a rescue dog.

leash

trainer

Sandy and Kim walk to the park. Sandy's *trainer* is there. A trainer is a kind of teacher. The trainer will train Sandy to find people who are lost.

Other people and their dogs are at the park. The trainer will teach Sandy and some other dogs.

It is time for Sandy's lesson. The trainer gives Kim his cap. Then the trainer hides.

Kim puts the cap in front of Sandy.
Sandy smells the cap.
The cap smells like the trainer.

"Find the trainer, Sandy," Kim says.
Sandy sniffs the air. She can smell the trainer! She pulls on her leash.

Kim takes off the leash.
"Go, Sandy!" she says. Sandy runs.
She passes a family.
She finds the trainer!

Kim gives Sandy a hug. "Good dog," she says. Kim is proud of Sandy. One day Sandy will help people. Sandy will help find people who are lost!